A Message From the Master

Inspired by God
Written by Deloris N. Harris

In Association with  *Columbus, Ohio*

A MESSAGE FROM THE MASTER
WHAT IS THE MESSAGE? THE WORD OF GOD

Copyright © 2004 by Deloris N. Harris.
All rights reserved.

ISBN 0-976-3689-0-0

Library of Congress Control Number: 2006924958

Published in association with Ambassador Press

Cover photo courtesy of istockphoto.com
Cover and interior design by Joe Eckstein
Imagine! Studios www.artsimagine.com

All rights reserved. No part of this publication may be reproduced or transmitted in any form or by any means, including informational storage and retrieval systems, without permission in writing from the author or publisher, except for brief quotations in a review.

All scripture quotations, unless otherwise indicated, are taken from the *Breakthrough Miracle Bible, King James Version.*

First Ambassador Press printing, April 2006

A MESSAGE FROM THE MASTER

Revelation 21:5

*And he that sat upon the throne said, behold,
I make all things new. And he said unto me,
write: for these words are true and faithful.*

"I thought these were poems, but God said they were messages for the people and I needed to share them."

WORD FOR LIFE

Psalm 68:11

The Lord gave the word: great was the company of those that published it.

2 Timothy 3:16

All scripture is given by inspiration of God and is profitable for doctrine, for reproof, for correction, for instruction in righteousness.

"God said these were not poems: they are messages for His people to let them know how much He loves us."

DEDICATION

To all those who are going through trials and tribulation, sickness and pain, heartache, or financial distress, the Lord, our God, is an awesome God. Trust and believe. If He said it, it will come to pass.

Be encouraged and know that He is God. He doesn't need anybody else. His Word is true and faithful.

He is the living Word, and His words are for you.

Hold on, have faith in God.

ACKNOWLEDGEMENT

First, "Glory be to God." Thanks for the gift and love you so freely give, for your grace and mercy forever and ever.

To all my brothers and sisters at Refuge Baptist Church, who believed that God was using me to inspire His people to believe that He is there all the time.

To Pastor Jones, a million thanks for believing in me and letting me read God's messages to the people on Sunday mornings.

Sister Jones, thanks for your encouragement and love and for believing in me. I miss you.

To Von Thomas and all the women at the ministry, for your prayers and support.

My best friend, Betty Croomer, who gave me that extra push.

A MESSAGE FROM THE MASTER

Pat Desmon, thanks for believing in me.

To my daughter, Demitrus Evans, for always believing that I could do it, knowing that I can do all things through Christ who strengthens me. Mechie, "I love you, Baby."

To my daughter, Dannell Harris, while going through the valley of the shadow of death, standing on God's Holy Word that He would heal her, and He did. "Thank you, Lord, Glory to your name." Nell, "I love you."

My wonderful son, Daniel Harris, Jr., who did not always agree with me about my thoughts but was still there for me and loved me in spite of it all, telling me that I could do it. Danny, "I love you."

Thanks to Kimmy and Kathy for helping me in every way possible and for your prayers.

Thanks to Ken Mosley for all his help.

Special thanks to Becky Knox, who gave so much of her extra time, giving me a helping hand and her love and friendship. "Love you".

Special thanks to Steve Sexton, who was just a Godsend.

Thanks to the late Christopher Reeve, who received the message that God spoke to me to send him. God will do what He said. May God forever bless and keep you.

To my dearest brother, Fred G. Evans (Tippie), who is waiting on God to come and take him to heaven. ("For the dead in Christ shall be the first to rise"). For the Word he preached to me and his love and encouragement. I miss you, but I will see you one day soon.

To my Pastor, Rod Parsley, for the Word that pierced my soul, helping to increase my faith. I believe that God can do abundantly more than we could ever ask for. Truly, there is nothing impossible with God.

Although I am thankful to all of you, this book is not about me but the one who has entrusted me to write it, JESUS CHRIST, my LORD and SAVIOR.

Therefore, I take no credit for the words, for they were spoken to me from Him who created me.

May GOD bless and keep all of you in His care forever.

INSPIRED BY GOD

"I want you to know that this is of GOD, for He uses me, His willing vessel, to speak to you through these words."

Revelation 2:7

*He that hath an ear, let him hear what
the Spirit said unto the church.*

When I first began to write these poems, I was asked to do "The Welcome" for my Pastor's anniversary. I said that I would but did not know where to begin. I had told God to use me in any way He wanted. So I prayed and asked God to help me prepare to do work for Him. Right away He said for me to get a pencil and paper. I did, and the words came from Him, as I began to write them down. I remember crying, worshipping and thanking God for being so awesome, for I know it is not me. It is a gift that He has given me, and I can only do it if He gives it to me.

A MESSAGE FROM THE MASTER

Occasionally I may be a little sleepy, but He will wake me up and tell me to get a pen and paper or He will just start speaking the words to me, and I will start writing them down. Sometimes it can be while I'm watching TV, reading, working, or even if someone is on my heart or on my mind. I have asked God to give me a word of encouragement for someone to rest on their heart because He knew what they were going through.

I recall one Sunday morning when getting ready for church, I was singing and praising Him (you know He loves that). And I said to Him, "God, I would like to send a couple of my poems in for a contest, so you let me know which ones to send in." Right away He told me which ones to enter. He also told me that theses were not poems but "messages" for His people and were to be shared, not just for me to keep to myself. Glory be to God, the Father, Son and Holy Ghost.

I hope that this book of messages that have been inspired by God will help you in some way.

TABLE OF CONTENTS

All the Way....................20
A Mother's Love....................19
Be Strong, My Sister....................21
But...GodLook at me now....................31
Dad – Father....................23
Excellent....................24
Father....................26
Father in Heaven....................28
Feeelings...Now....................31
Feelings...When....................31
Goodness of Jesus....................32
Hear Me....................34
I Am of Glory....................36
I Know Who You Are....................38
I Sent....................40
I Will Heal....................42
Let Me Tell....................45
Look at Me....................46
Love Is Not Gone....................48
May Be Your Call....................50
My Brother....................52
My Child....................55
My Gift to You in Times of Trouble....................56
My Servant....................58
My Sister....................61
My Sweet Sister....................62
Our God....................64
Rejoice....................66
Sisters from Heaven above....................69

Son..70
Stan.......................................72
Star Bright 73
Sunday Prayer 74
"Sweetie"..................................75
Thank You, Lord 76
The Man 79
The Old Rugged Cross 80
The Reason for the Season................81
Truth to Tell.............................82
Waiting...................................84
Welcome..................................85
Welcome..................................86
Welcome II...............................87
Who Are You? 88
Will You Come?........................90
Your Friend 97
You and Me 92
You Are My Friend 94
You Are Not Alone 96

Special Delivery........................99

A MOTHER'S LOVE

When I think of the woman who brought me into this world,
    lying with pain and suffering,
    that's my friend.
A glimpse, a smile, and after bringing me in, she
    thanked her God for her newborn friend.

She held me tight in her arms and kissed my forehead
    and promised I'll never leave you alone.
She watched me grow every step of the way, pain
    and suffering, but she never went away.

I went off to school; a phone call away.
I could count on my mother, for she never went away.

Now I'm grown, on my own, and now I'm
    a mother, always here to stay.
But you see, I'm not unwise, she's here today, and
    someday my God will take her away.

So if you have a mother, be kind, loving and strong,
    for a good mother will never leave you alone.

ALL THE WAY

When I have a problem and don't know what to say,
God opens the door and leads me all the way.

He tells me I am His child. He is loving, kind and strong.
He holds my hand when I am worried,
   and He tells me where I belong.

He wipes away my tears when I think everything is wrong.
He wakes me in the morning and gives me a sweet song.

He carries me throughout my day so I am sure
   He loves me. He loves me all the way.

He is my Father, our God, the Son and Holy Ghost.
So let Him guide you with his loving
   mercy and lead you all the way.

BE STRONG, MY SISTER

God loves you with all His might;
Whatever you do hold on real tight.
It's okay to be happy and sometimes sad.
He says we must put away the past.

So go on and live, but put your hand in His
and learn to forgive.
He will see that you will always live.

Your earthly father is gone, but your Heavenly Father lives on.
Give him a chance, and He will make you strong.

Remember: to know Him is to love Him.
He loves you still.

DAD – FATHER

My dad made me and then he left me.
He never called or wrote. He never knocked or rang
   a bell, but he went about his business I can tell.

He didn't clothe or feed me; no love he gave at all.
 I thought he was my dad, but he cared nothing at all.

But you see, I have a Father who loves me dearly.
He says that I can call Him and He's never busy,
   not at all.
I tell Him all my troubles and He lets me
   know He cares.
He says "If I'll be faithful and keep His Holy word,
He'll take me up to Heaven to live with the angels."

If you don't know my Father, just give Him a try.
He'll love you as He loves me, and you'll
   never have to cry.

EXCELLENT

I, the Lord, am bringing my spiritual women
    out to let you know that you are of me,
    worthy to be excellent in all ways and
    in everything that you do.

This is the time to turn your life around to do good
    and gracious work. I want you to listen
    and hear my word and what I have planned for your life.

You're my beloved children, women of
    the Highest God. Hear me!
    Listen to the words, let them seep into in
    your heart, your mind and soul.

I do this because I have blessed you to
    become gracious in my sight.
    Whatever you do, look to things above that
    you may be blessed in heavenly places.

I have gathered you here to praise my name, to open your
    mind, to receive the word I have sent.
    I am waiting here in Heaven for you. I love you and surely
    you want to come home
    and live with my Father and me.

The door is open for you who will receive
    my love and my ways for you.
    Come to me if you need perfect rest.

I have sent the Word. Hold on, be still and continue
    to do my will: "You must do it right."

FATHER

There's a Father we all can share;
He is here with you and me. He is everywhere.

He forgives our sins and gives us complete peace within.

He loves us so, this we all should know.
He is a friend like no other. He is closer to us than any brother.

He wipes away the tears from your eyes,
And lets you know He is standing by.

He is at the door with His arms stretched wide,
Waiting on you to let go of your pride.

He came to this world to set us free,
So that He could save you and me.

He loves us all the time. His love is more
   precious than silver and gold.
Don't you think this is the Father that you should know?

I thank Him for being a friend of mine,

Holding me and keeping me straight and "in line."
If I need Him, He is always there.
He carries the load when I have had more than my share.

All my life I wanted someone to love me that way,
Now I have Him with me, and He will never go away.

He is looking to give you the love He gives to me.
Open the door and just receive.

He loves you, and He knows the pain and aches we share.
He is willing to take it all, but we must leave it there.

FATHER IN HEAVEN

While in the air I thought of you
The clouds were gray
a little sunny and blue.

I thought of the things that you have done,
I want you to know I love everyone.
A flight up high made me realize
that you are beyond the sky.

A little bumpy, the plane would rock,
but I know that you would be there as quick as I can knock.
I can see you there with your arms open wide.
I tell you, Father, when it comes to you, I have no pride.

I thank you for taking me here and there,
for bringing me and letting me share,
such peace and contentment you gave to me,
I wish everyone could see just how sweet you can be.

Before I landed on the ground below,
the sun came out with the prettiest glow.
I know you were there watching over me
because you're the one who set me free.

Father, I thank you for being my friend,
loving and caring for me until the end,
so as I close I want you to know,
Father in Heaven,
I love you so.

FEELINGS...WHEN

I was a child, happy but sad.
I was a teen, happy but sad.
I was a young adult, happy but sad.
I was grown, happy but awfully sad.
I am older, very happy but sad.

FEEELINGS...NOW

I looked over my life and what did I see,
straight ahead of me.

BUT...GOD
LOOK AT ME NOW.

I am somebody, wait and see.
I am somebody because God loves me.
I am somebody but maybe not what I should be.
I am somebody, just look at me.
I am somebody, I hope and pray.
I am somebody: God showed me the way.

A MESSAGE FROM THE MASTER

GOODNESS OF JESUS

If it were not for the goodness of Jesus, who died on Calvary,
the good that he did when he set my soul free.

If it were not for his goodness and mercy, my
soul would not be heavenly bound.
If it were not for his goodness that he turned my soul around,
I would be like that old ship at sea and could not be found.

If it were not for his goodness, that he
hung up on that old cross,
when he took away my burdens and said I was no longer lost

If it were not for his goodness, that he carried the load I bore,
what would I be? What would I dare,
if he had not showed how much he cared.

Just know today that his goodness is with you and me.
It's with us everywhere. Where else would he be?

So don't take it lightly. He did not have to care
and give us his goodness that only God in heaven can share.

Look all around, His goodness is here and there.
His goodness is life for you and me.
I love Him because He cares, and He set my soul free.

A MESSAGE FROM THE MASTER

HEAR ME

I come again to let you know, my children, how I love you so.
But you do not receive my love; you won't
    even listen to your Father above.

I sent the Word. You have the book.
I asked you once again to take a good look.

I do not understand what's wrong with you.
I died so that you may be free, but you still do not worship me.

Open your ears to hear me out. They are
    not of me, the things you do.
I am not up here sleeping. I am watching you.
If you keep on going the way that you do,
    I want to be around to help you.

Fall on your knees and ask for forgiveness right away.
If you come back I will guide you my way.

You want to know who does she thinks she is?
She came to me at the end of her end, and she
    prayed that I would be her best friend.

She said use me Lord in every way.
I gave her my words, but you keep turning them away.

I want you to know that I am coming soon. I will turn
    my back and won't even acknowledge you.
I told you in the book that my ways are not your
    ways and my thoughts are not your thoughts.
This is one of the things you cannot figure
    out. I am still waiting on your call.
My arms are open, and the door is too. I am
    the only one who can restore you.

Jesus

A MESSAGE FROM THE MASTER

I AM OF GLORY

Glory, glory, glory be, Luther,
   as you know Satan, used to live with me.
He was the prettiest angel you ever did see.

He never had to feel your pain,
   or worry about working or anything.
But he thought he was mighty and tough;
   he wanted to be God, instead of me.

I always loved him and always cared,
   but he would not listen—he just got that bad.
So one day I had to kick him out.
   He took some others with him and turned them out.
Now he lives on earth with you.
   Don't you let him devour you too.

He came to seek and destroy
   because he cannot come back to all this peace and joy.
Hell is where he will always be.

So put your armor on and stand still, be strong.
   I will be coming to take you home.

Do not let him show his face, kick him out.
> Do not let him win your race.

He will try to sneak and take your place.
> He would like to lead you where he will be.

Rebuke, rebuke, rebuke him I say.
> He is after you, don't you turn away.

He is busy doing all that he can:
> To take you to hell is his demand.

I am looking and watching everything that is done.
> I am the Lord and I love everyone.

Choose the right way to go.
> Will it be heaven or hell? Do you know?

I am that I am: your Lord, your King
> and your Savior for life.

Start worshipping me,
> Whatever you do, no one else can restore you.

A MESSAGE FROM THE MASTER

I KNOW WHO YOU ARE

I know you, better than you know me. You see,
I formed you and placed you in your mother's womb.
I molded you and gave you my touch.
I shaped you because I love you so much.
It is time for you to seek me out, I am always
here. I am just waiting on you.

Daniel, my son, I want you to know that I am
your Lord and how much I love you so.
I hear you cry. You can wipe your eyes;
all you need to do it let go of your pride.
Call me, call me I say. I am listening for
you, and I am just standing by.
You have my word; it's in the book,
Don't waste time. Hurry and take that look.

I will help you through it all and all you
have to do is give me a call.
I love you. I love you. What else do I have to do?
I am your Father, and I am depending on you.

I know you don't understand what's really going on,
But I am the one who can make you strong. It's not too late.
I can use you today, but you must not make the same mistake.

I have sent you a word that I am your
Father. I will never leave you alone.
All I ask is that you come on home.
The world is moving a little too fast.
People are not listening; they are just passing on by.
I am calling on you to get things right.
I am waiting on you both day and night.
I can help you if you give me a try. I am the
one who made you, and I am standing by.

Look over your life and tell me what you see.
Yes, I am the one who wants you to always be with me.
Call on me; I am here to listen.
I will walk you where you need to be;
if only you listen to me.

Daniel, do you know your name is in the Book?
Would you read it and take that look?
Smile, for it's you and me; tell me what do you see?
I am waiting to get you straight, and I am here.
I love you, isn't that great?

Always remember I am your Father. I am your best
friend. Let's be thick together until the end.

Your Father

I SENT

God sent this woman for us this day
He sent a place to worship and pray
He sent a place to sit right down,
For us, my sisters, to come all around.

He is letting us know that He loves us so.
He is coming back; He is coming to town,
And when He comes back,
He wants us to wear a long white gown.

He said He knows we are traveling the way
To tell you He is with us in every way.
He said to keep doing His will
And be still, still, still.

The woman He sent is doing His work.
She has nothing but peace and contentment
Because she knows why she was sent

The door is open for us today.
Whatever we do, stay on the right way.
Time is passing very quickly.

He will be back in a hurry.
He does not need us, but we need Him
Come, my children, let's get ready to live with Him

He knows your pains, worries and cares.
He is always with us—each burden He shares.
We may not think He is with us, but He is everywhere
He will meet us and carry our load, but we must leave it there

Call on Him, for we are all in need.
Jesus is in Heaven with our Father, and He hears our pleas.
For we must not worry and we must not fret.
Our Father has never left us yet.

Look up to Heaven and thank Him every day,
for He will soon be coming our way
He will never leave you or forsake you.
He will give you strength and help you to be strong
He will walk you through to where you belong
I promise to supply all you need.

Your Heavenly Father

A MESSAGE FROM THE MASTER

I WILL HEAL

I, the Lord, who raised Lazarus from the dead,
Who asked you to read and meditate on my Word,
I have the power, to strengthen and heal,
If only you would do my Holy will.

Where is your trust and your faith? I tell you this,
I took your place.
I died on Calvary a long time ago,
That you might live and have peace as you go.

I carried the load to set you free,
That one day you would live with me.
If you think you're not strong, lean on me,
I'll help you along.

Open the book to see what I have to say:
I tell you I am with you every day.
Don't worry about what to do—just trust and pray.
I will see you through.

My power is from heaven above;
Just seek me and receive my love.

You don't have to be sick any given day,
For I, the Lord, don't want you to be that way.

If you are weak, I will make you strong,
All I ask is come back where you belong.
I can heal you from head to foot,
Just read the Word and take a look.

Pray in faith, whatever you do,
I am your Lord, and I want you to know that I love you.
I don't want you to be weak, sick and in pain,
I will stretch out my hands and heal you again.

But you must believe that I died for you.
Trust me, hold on whatever you do.
My words are life for you; listen, read, trust, meditate,
Have faith, I am speaking to you.

JESUS

What would Jesus say if he were here with me?
He would probably say, "Don't worry, I come to set you free."

What would Jesus say if he were here with me?
He would probably say, "Lean over here on me."

What would Jesus say if he were here with me?
He would probably say, "I am waiting, waiting on you today."

What would Jesus say if he were here with me?
He would probably say, "Here I am. I
  am everything you need."

What would Jesus say if he were here with me?
He would probably say, "Come, my son, come, my daughter,
  I have blessed you. Now let it be."

Deloris N. Harris

LET ME TELL

Let me tell you something you should know
About my Father who loves you so.

He died on Calvary a long time ago.
He died for you and He died for me.
He died that all men might be free.

He walked this earth so we could see
How much He loved us and He came to set us free.

LOOK AT ME

My child, my child, can't you see
    that mean old devil is after you?
    My Father in heaven has sent you to me
    to let you know that you are free.

Don't you worry and don't you fret. I,
    the Lord, have never left you yet.
    You must flee from all that is wrong. Just
    leave it, and I will walk you along.

I know you are hurting and full of pain.
    I told you I can heal you again.

Peace of mind is what you need,
    come back my child and be set free.
    Don't think for a moment that I am mad,
for I love you. Take that and be glad.

I know you think you have turned your back on me.
    Call me up, and we will see.

My child, I thought I would let you know
    that I am the one and only one who loves you so.
My word is in the Book. Seek and find me—take a closer look.

I want you to know I am with you everywhere you go,
    for I am right here—I will open the door.

Come back to me. I will set you free,
    and you can be close with me.

Love,
Jesus

A MESSAGE FROM THE MASTER

LOVE IS NOT GONE

God said it's all right to let him go.
He will give him back.
You may grieve, but joy you will receive.

I gave him for awhile. He was mine,
and I let you share.
I took him back—that's how much I care.

You are my child, and I know it is hard.
Just remember I am still with you in every part.

Life will go on; hold on and be strong.
I will be with you where you belong.
Take time to remember and smile.
He is in Heaven with me, my child.

I will heal you in every place,
Just keep me in your heart and mind.
I am with you all the time.

Come to me if you're ever in need.
I will take the pain, and I will bleed.

I love you: this I want you to know
I am your Lord. I love you so.

I have been with you more than you know.
You take me with you where you go.
Time will heal your broken heart.
We will be watching you from heaven above.
We will always cherish your love.

I just want you to know that I am all right.
I am in heaven with my Father, my love.
Stay sweet—we will soon meet.

Live your life. It is not that long,
For God gave you this time to linger along.

I love you, My Sweet.

A MESSAGE FROM THE MASTER

MAY BE YOUR CALL

Softly and tenderly Jesus is calling for
   you and me to come home.
He's standing at the door with his arms open wide,
   waiting on you to let go of your pride.

Let me tell you the story of our God and His glory.
Up on a cross He suffered, bled and died
   that we might have joy, peace, and love
   and live on the other side.
Oh, you may say there's no life after death,
   but listen my brother and sister,
   if there were not, He would have told us so.
He left us his Word. It is in the Book (the Bible).
   Pick it up—words for your life. Try reading it tonight.

You see, I too was lost in this world of sin. I
   did not find Jesus, but he found me.
   He took me in and set me free.
I was looking for love in all the wrong places.
   It was not my father or mother, nor my sister or brother,
But it was Jesus who has always loved and was there for me.
   Even when I did not know, he carried
   the load. He took the pain.

He gave me back my life again. He loves you,
    as he does me if you go to him and let it be.

He will give you new life and take away
    your burdens and set you free.
    God is an awesome God, he loves you very much.
Do you feel him tugging at your heart? He's
    been waiting on you from the start.

You may say, I will think on this another day,
    maybe tomorrow, but tomorrow may be too late.
You may say, who does she think she is?
    I was lost, sinking in sin, but Jesus loves me and took me in.

Your Sister in Christ Jesus

A MESSAGE FROM THE MASTER

MY BROTHER

Just a few words I must say today,
I want you to know you are my brother in Christ,
    And I love you so.
We are his children and must obey.
He gave me favor with you one day.
He said to tell you what I need to do
That you would do it right straight through.
He gave you, my brother, to cherish as of this day
I will never forget you.
Thanks to God, He sent you my way.
I know you do not understand,
But one day you will see that
    He loves you, as He loves me.
He says He has a plan for your life.
It may not be what you want, but it will be all right.
Know that nothing is impossible for Him.
He will always be with you.
He will never let you stray.
You may not do all you should right now,
But He will open your eyes and guide you to do His will.
Just remember, my brother, I say this to
    you on this very special day,
God loves you, and He cares.

He will never, never leave you
    For He's just that way.
So as I close this message to you,
Know for sure He will use you,
As He does us all. Just say yes,
    And you will be okay.

MY CHILD

I birthed my child into this world of sin.
 I tried to be her first friend.
She went away to school, not far from home.
She wanted to be near her mother,
 for that's where she belongs.
But as time passed, she went away.
She tried real hard but had to go her own way.

I love and care for her and what she does.
 She grew to be the lady God wanted her to be.
With God in her life she will be strong;
His love and mercy will never lead her wrong.

She loves me, loves me very much.
For my child is Demitrus, with the tender touch.

Love,
Mom

MY GIFT TO YOU IN TIMES OF TROUBLE

In times of trouble when you need a friend,
I want you to know I'm here to the end.

When you need a shoulder,
Mine are as wide as the world;
    Leave your worries and pains there.

Call on me if you are ever in need.
I'll carry the load, and if you need, I'll also bleed.

Trust in me whatever you do.
I want you to know I'm here for you.

I'm your Father in Heaven above.
I love you with my unconditional love.

I will listen, and I will carry the load.
I promise I'll be with you wherever you go.

So take heed to my every word.
I'm here when you call, just give me the words—
    I will take it all.

You say you believe me. Show me your faith:
leave it in my hands; I will take your place.

Wipe your eyes, dry up your tears.
I'm right here, for I love you, my dear.

Love you,
Jesus

A MESSAGE FROM THE MASTER

MY SERVANT

I sent a man from the hills of PA.
I sent this man to be with you today.
I called on him to give you my word,
To tell of my goodness and love for you.

You still have not received him
   the way that you should,
So I am giving you a second chance to do My Servant good.
This is my man. He came to give my word.
 Listen, whatever you do, take time to receive these words,
   for they come from me.

Hell is where you all will be.
If you don't listen, I'll leave you be.
The time is near, just look around.
   What do you see?
 I tell you, I'm coming to town.

I sit high and look low.
I see what you do, and I watch where you go.
If you think this is a play thing, get out of my way.
I tell you, I'll leave you as quickly as the day.

Deloris N. Harris

You don't worship and praise me like you should.
I tell you that's just no good.
Don't think you can come and pretend each day.
I know your spirit, and it's not right any given day.

Just listen—each word is true.
I want you to know that I, the Lord, love you.

MY SISTER

I saw you yesterday with your bright
eyes and your little lost smile,
You were kind of down and could not sit for awhile.

You didn't know who to talk to, so you walked for awhile.
You walked so long it was almost a mile.

You thought, "What's wrong with me?
I know someone who takes care of me."
You looked above to Heaven and said,
"My God has been with me all the time."

So you turned back around and went on your way,
With a smile as big as a bright sunny day!

See, God is with you every step of the way.

A MESSAGE FROM THE MASTER

MY SWEET SISTER

My Sister, my Sister,
Just want to let you know,
how very much I love you so.
When I was down, had no peace within,
Our God showed you and told you to take me in.
You obeyed and took me under your wings,
that I may find the peace that I need.
I thank Him for loving me so much,
for letting me be close to someone so dear.
I thank you for sharing your thoughts
and love you have for Him,
For He is the one who sent me here.
I did not know you that well but I loved
you deep down in my heart.
Now I know why He placed me here,
so you could encourage me,
And be close and near to your heart.
I do not know what the future holds,
but my love for you will always be told.
God is awesome, awesome, indeed, for
I know He has set me free.
I may not be the finest person in the world but I Love You.
God knows this; that's why I can tell.

So as we share our hopes and dreams of His mercy and love,
I know He carries the load to help us bear.
This is just a little message to say,
Sister, I Love you in every way.
Peace be with you always, especially today.
God loved us so much that He gave His son,
That we would have peace and love for everyone.
I am here with you as long as He allows me to be.
Come to me if there's anything I can do.

Just a little message to say
"I Love You."

OUR GOD

Let me tell you about a man I know
He sits high, and he looks low.
He is Jesus Christ, our Lord and Savior.

He loves you, as he loves me.
He has no favored child, as you can see.
He is standing at the door with his arms open wide,
Waiting on you to let go of your pride.

You say you are not happy. You don't have to be.
For he is love—that's the way it is supposed to be.

His love is here for you today.
All you have to do is see things his way.
You don't have to worry, and you sure don't have to fret:
Our God in heaven has never left you yet.

REJOICE

I went to sleep with Jesus on my mind.
He woke me up feeling just fine.
He gave me this word to give to you:

The spirit of the Lord is upon me. You are
in the presence of the highest God.
He would love for you to worship and praise his holy name,
for he is the one who woke you this morning, gave you life
and brought you over the highways with
his blessed traveling mercy.

He is the one who opens the door for you
all through your life. He wants you to rejoice and praise
him, for he is worthy. This day he is giving to you, to have
peace and happiness and to feel his presence in his house.

You did not come here by accident. He brought you here,
as he has brought you here and there so many times
before. Give him His glory and honor that is due him.
I truly welcome you in the name of Jesus Christ
our Lord and Savior of this world.

You have a savior who cares, waits for you with His arms stretched wide open, ready and willing to do whatever you need to help you along the way, this day and every day of your life.

Remember this day, for you are more than welcome…you are loved.

"Praise God" You are more than welcome.

Deloris N. Harris

SISTERS FROM HEAVEN ABOVE

Love is my Sister, whoever she may be.
She has no color; she's just my Sister and me.

We love each other; we think something alike.
We know that our Heavenly Father loves us,
   so we hold on real tight.

I see you come to church with
   your family, holding hands.
You know that I love you, and we greet wherever we stand.

Your eyes are as bright and sweet as the morning light.
You always have a smile and something sweet to say,
I know you are my Sister; we both feel the same way.

We may not be born from the same woman,
But our Father is the same in Heaven.
We share His love, but most of all we share His blood.

So I'm giving you this, my Sister, just to say
   we're total Sisters from Heaven above.
I want you to know you mean so much
   to me: it's my Sister and me.

SON

My son, God sent you to me, for at that
time I was as down as could be.
I needed you to help ease the pain, for I
was suffering and so ashamed.
I called on God to give me a son;
I remember they killed His only one:
The one who saved me, his name is Jesus, the love of my life.
He wants you to know it's going to be all right.

He's molded you in His hands for your life to
be sweet and sensitive as you are indeed.
He let you go your own way, but now is
your time to see things His way.
Call on him. He's waiting to hear the words
He gave you before you were even here.
He sent you here for me to love and tell
you, you were sent from above.

Your earthly father did not do you right, but
God's hands of love will show you the light.
He wants you to know how much He loves you
too. Come unto him; He's waiting for you.
His love will walk you along. All you

have to do is come on home.
Your home was in heaven, before the one here on earth.
Trust Him. I know He will do good work.

It's time for you to be free. All he asks is that you trust.
He knows your struggle and your pain. Call
on him, he can heal you today.
Read His words; they're in the Book of
Life. Pick it up, do it tonight.
Read and ask him. He wants to see you through.

I tell you this so you will know, He loves
you so, and He will never let you go.
Peace you will find, His heart is straight and always on time.
He wants you to know wherever you go, He'll be with you.
Just watch what He does. He's going to show you.

My son, I'm writing this to say He will always be with you.
He's just that way.

Love,
Mom

STAN

My nephew had a problem. I thank God he's all right.
He did not know who to talk to, so he read the Holy Word.
He went to his mother. At the time she did not understand.
She could not handle the problem, and Stan took off and ran.

He ran from the devil, who chased Stan here and there,
but God was with him and showed him that he cared.
He sent down his light from heaven to show
    him the way—it was all right.
He held him in his arms and stayed there with him all night.
They found him in the morning,
    all bruised and cut and worn.
But his spirit was not broken, for God
    loved him and God cared.

So if you have a problem, take it to the Lord in prayer.
    Hold on to his kindness and his unchanging hand,
    for He is with you, with you wherever you stand.

Deloris N. Harris

STAR BRIGHT

One night a star in the East was shining so bright,
God had sent down His Holy light.

The wise men from afar came so near,
To see the baby Jesus who loves us so dear.

Presents of gold, incense and myrrh
Were given at the Savior baby's birth.

For this is the Savior who owns the earth.
He was sent from heaven with one great love for all mankind,
Who are in desperate need.

He reins over the earth, the sky and sea.
He is the Savior born for you and me.

He came to earth to take away our sins,
That one day we would live in heaven with him.

So as we celebrate, being merry as we play,
Don't forget to kneel down and pray,
For Christ, our Savior, came to us on Christmas Day.

SUNDAY PRAYER

I go to church on Sunday to sing, worship and pray
I read the Holy Bible to see what God has to say.

I listen to the preacher to hear God's Holy Word,
And then I thank him for that very special day.

So get up on Sunday morning and go to church your way.
Kneel down to God and thank Him you are able to pray.

God loves you, and He is listening to every word you say.
He knows that we are sinners, and He
   wants to lead us His way.

So just be glad you have a Father who cares for you all the way.

"SWEETIE"

So you think you have a "sweetie"
Who caresses with every touch.
So you think that he loves you,
You think he loves you much

He comes and goes when he wants
A kiss, a smile or touch

Well, let me tell you something
Your "sweetie" is not like mine,
For my "sweetie" is with me.
He's with me all the time.

He lets me know he cares.
He's with me everywhere.
He takes me, and he holds me.
My Jesus is the one who cares.

A MESSAGE FROM THE MASTER

THANK YOU, LORD

Use me up, Lord, whatever you do.
    use me until my time is through.
If I need a cleaning, do it with care.
    Let me stay in your arms and keep me there.

I don't know why you are so sweet to me.
    I'm just a sinner who's thanking you, Lord, for saving me.

I remember when I was lost, I did not know you were there,
    But you let me know that you are everywhere.
I thank you for caring and looking after me.
    Thank you, Lord, for setting me free.

Lord, you have given me so much peace.
    I thank you for such sweet release.
Lord, I take you with me wherever I go;
    you are in my mind, my heart and soul.
I look to Heaven because I know you are there,
    I can hardly wait to meet you there.

I know that Heaven is a beautiful place,
    for I can look around and see all the

beauty you have set before me.
Your love is so warm, and you're so gentle to me.
    I am so very glad that my Lord, you love me.

Lord, Lord, Lord, whatever you do, stay with me.
    keep me strong but most of all keep
    letting me know where I belong.
I will hold on and keep cherishing your love, mercy and grace.
    I am so sure you want it that way.
My Lord, I am thanking you for this day,
    for caring, watching over me and
    holding me all along the way.

I love you Lord. I just want to say
    thank you, thank you for everyday.

Deloris N. Harris

THE MAN

I know a man who is tall as a tree,
And he looks down on little old me.

I know a man who is tall and strong.
He lets me know where I belong.

I know a man mighty and tough
He loves me and you very much.

I know a man who is Lord and Savior,
And gives me life without any measure.

THE OLD RUGGED CROSS

He died on a hill called Calvary,
A cross he bore all alone.
I wish I could have been there,
Although I am not strong.

He died for me, and he died for you,
If you had a cross, what would you do?

Would you die for me? Would you forgive my sins?
Wouldn't it be nice if we could all be like him?

Could I suffer for what you've done?
I don't think so, not even one.
Yet I say I love you. Yes, I love, indeed,
But I am not the one who died on Calvary.

So love your enemies and love your brothers,
For we do have a cross to bear, maybe not on the hill,
But it will be Calvary.

THE REASON FOR THE SEASON

My brothers and sisters, where would you be
    if my Father had not sent me to you?
Would you be weary, torn and worn if He
    had not stretched out His arm?

I come to set you free, that you may sit
    with my Father and me.
He sent his love, all wrapped in a manger that
    you may be kept from harm and danger

I stand at the door with arms open wide, ready
    to receive you if you let go of your pride.

So, come to me and be set free, to live in
    heaven with the Father and Me.

Jesus

TRUTH TO TELL

Let me tell you a story about a man I know,
He is with you and me everywhere we go.

One day my daughter got sick. She was full of fever and pain,
thrush in her mouth.
So sick she could not hold her head up or hardly stand.
She went to the doctor to get some help,
He said she had a disease no one could cure.

He gave her medicine to prolong her life,
But you see I know who could hold her tight.
I worried and worried; that did us no good,
So I prayed and cried and wondered why?

You see God so lovingly opened my eyes.
My heart was aching, not able to rest.
Tears in the morning, noon and night,
I called on the Lord for help.

I said to Him,
"God, you who raised Lazarus from the dead.
You can save her life."
I gave it to Him and left it there.

Now my daughter is well and in His care,
We gave it to Jesus. He made everything all right.
I know that he loves us so we're holding
on for the rest of our life.

WAITING

I am still with you in heart.
There is nothing that could ever tear us apart.
God chose today to take me away.
I know you are sad.
Lean on God.
He will walk with you all the way.
You know, my dear,
You're the best thing that ever happened to me,
But our Father had plans before this day
That we would meet and share our lives and love one another.
You must be strong and live on,
For God will take you too
And bring you home.
I will be watching you with our Lord
And love you as from the start,
For we will soon meet again,
But while you are waiting,
Go ahead and bloom.
You are the one Rose
God gave to me
Because He knew you would be as sweet as can be.
Take this word from me today:
I love you!
I love you!
For God will be with you in every way
And throughout everyday.

Love you, my dear!

WELCOME

W — Wonderful is His name
E — Enter into His gates
L — Love the Lord, thy God
C — Come in and Worship Him
O — One and only Savior
M — Mother for the motherless
E — Eternity is ours forever

Put them together– WELCOME in My Father's House

A MESSAGE FROM THE MASTER

WELCOME

This is the day that the Lord has made
He wants to welcome you in His presence
To sing, worship and praise His Holy Name.

This building is called Refuge,
Meaning shelter or protection from harm,
A place one may turn to for relief or help.

But most of all this is the House of the Lord,
Who has made us to praise Him.

So as I welcome you in the name of our Lord Jesus Christ.
May you be blessed and fulfilled in all that is done here
in the name of Jesus.
You are more than welcome.

WELCOME II

I was asked to do the welcome, and I
did not know what to say,
But I thank my God that He brought you along the way.

You did not have to come here.
You could have gone another way.
But my God is awesome; He led you here today.

So I thank Him for his kindness and
His love He shared so bright.
I welcome you here that you may get a blessing
from God who sits on high.

The door is always open for you, whether near or far away,
So please stop back by Refuge and sing, worship and pray.

You are welcome.

WHO ARE YOU?

I met you a year ago.
I did not know you or where to go.

I was trying to be nice.
I did not even think twice,
For God let me know that
It was all right.

I dropped you off with blessings from God.
I started to think but did not let it sink.

I did not see you for awhile.
I was not in touch,
But I thought of you and did smile.

I did not know what it would be,
For a man of God to notice me.
Time has passed and we crossed by the path.

God led us here to seek and find,
If there may be a special line.

I do not know where this will go.
I put my faith upon His hand,
And who's to know if you are the man?

A MESSAGE FROM THE MASTER

WILL YOU COME?

God is waiting on you today, waiting for you to find the way.
There is already a path for you. He has left the Book,
   If you would only seek and take a good look.

What are you searching for? Do you really know?
   You have two choices, which way will you go?

All He asks is live as Jesus did.
   Is that so hard when He has already forgiven?

Where is your loyalty, is it to man or God?
Whom will you follow?
I think you know where it starts.
For God is awesome, awesome indeed.
He will show you. He gives to all who plead.

He died for you, up on the cross. He was
   wounded for your transgression.
His bruises for your inadequacies, and the
   chastisement of your peace was upon Him.
And what about his stripes? That you may be healed?

If I were you, I would not have to think twice;
I would run to Him; I would give Him my life.
When I think of God and all He means to me,
Sometimes I am so speechless, speechless as can be.
For who could love me the way that He does?
It is a mystery, only from God above.

He is always my shelter when I am in a storm.
He is the one who holds me and keeps me warm.
I call on Him for I know He is near.
Yes, my Jesus is the one that I love so dear.
I tell you this so you will know, my Lord, my
    Savior Jesus Christ, I love you so.
Come to Him; His arms are open wide.
Listen, my brothers and sisters, let go of your pride.

YOU AND ME

It's something about togetherness—God wants us to be.
He brought you here like He brought little old me.

He put us in a building and sat us down,
To worship and praise Him all around.

There is no color, just you and your friends,
Just think about what He is doing within.

God says, Look around at all of you,
See I'm bringing you love, love from me.

Take your sisters by the hand
And let everyone know just where you stand.

So love each other, whether little or tall,
Then you'll know I love you all.

You are my children, so let it be.
You are here only to worship and praise me.

YOU ARE MY FRIEND

I met you in a quiet setting of God.
I never knew you or where to start.
We were hurting with pain, unable to speak,
But God gave us such sweet release.

You were anxious and overjoyed to know
That our God loved you so.
He wants you to have peace and contentment within.
He let you know that I was to be your new friend.

We cried and shared, the hidden parts
that had been taken away.
God let us know that He loved us, so it was okay.

We can uplift each other in times of grief
Because God is in the midst of our need.
We can call and talk three, maybe four times a day.
Believe me, God wants it that way.

God is molding and shaping us to see,
The women He wants us to be.
I think of you every day,
For my God says it's okay.
We need each other to be strong,
God has planted us where we belong.

I think about my friends who were few and far between.
I want you to know, my friend, that I love you.

Now is the time to share what God has given us:
Peace, love and joy.
To read and pray, for God is on His way.
He wants us to reach out and tell of what He has done
And the love He has for everyone.

He said share His goodness with everyone
who has a broken heart,
Tell of the love while here on earth, what
He has in store for us in his heart.
And where He wants us to be when we depart.

He says love and cherish the ones I sent you,
For they are your friends when no one else is with you but me.

He is right here with you and me,
To let us know we are His children wherever we go,
To come together in times of need, to
comfort and to take heed.
To come together whatever we do,
For He is watching over you. So I am
telling you my sister, my friend,
I am here with you until the end.

A MESSAGE FROM THE MASTER

YOU ARE NOT ALONE

When the winds and storms are raging
and you cannot see the light,
I want you to know I am with you all
throughout the tough and windy nights.
Storms will hit my people, and you won't
always understand what is going on.
You must believe I am here with you,
and I will walk you along.
Just hold your head up; I will make you strong.
I will rest at night with you, as the tears roll down your face.
The day will come; the sun will shine,
and the tears will be washed away.
I did not say he would be on earth forever.
You knew I must take him home one day.
The life you had was wonderful.
Now I must fill the empty space.
Just look up to heaven.
He will be here waiting on you.
So do your work on earth,
and I will call you to meet with him soon.
I love you!
I will be with you everyday.

Jesus

YOUR FRIEND

I am writing you this letter to let you know
    that this is my child, not a show.
She came to me with love in her heart and asked
    me to use her, right from the start.
She said I'm here, whenever you need me
    to do, use me Lord, I'm coming to you.
I will give the word, just as you say, for
    I was yours, even before this day.
I am saying this to let you know the word
    she gives is coming from me.

If you are worried, down and think you are out,
just call me up, and I will turn you around.
This is not for show or play; I am with all of you everyday.
I sent you the word to read my book, but some
    of you still haven't taken a look.

I am trying to give you my word for
    life, why don't you try me?
I am your only friend in this hurting world. I
    am the one who can save your life.
I tell you what you do is not okay. I want
    you to live, just see it my way.
Time is short, and soon it will end. I'm telling
    you, I'm your Lord, your best friend!

Jesus

SPECIAL DELIVERY

One Thursday evening after work, while sitting in my doctor's office, waiting to be seen and reading a good book, I looked over the table in the waiting room and noticed all these magazines: *Life, Ebony, People,* and others. So I got up and there was this *Life Magazine* with Christopher Reeve in his wheelchair with his dog beside it.

You see, as a child, all my life I can remember loving Superman. He was Clark Kent, and I was Lois Lane. People used to call me Lois, short for Deloris. Anyway, I would always say Superman could fly me to the moon—that was fantastic.

I picked up that issue of *Life* and started to read the article about him. As I was reading, a voice said to me, "Write him." So I looked around, and I was the only one left there in the room. Again, the voice said, "Write him."

I said, "God, are you talking to me?"

He said, "Write him. I said, Write him."

I said, "God, I don't know how to get in touch with this man."

He said, "At the end of the article there is an address."

A MESSAGE FROM THE MASTER

I did not finish reading, but I just turned to the end, and there was the address of the Chistopher Reeve Foundation. After that God did not say anything else.

Then on Saturday morning while cleaning my apartment, the Lord spoke again and said, "Sit down and write him." So I grabbed a piece of computer paper and a pen and started to write. I said, "God, I don't know what to say to him." He said, "Tell him I will heal." Then He said, "Give him the testimony of your daughter," so I said, "Okay."

As I continued to write, He said, "Take a picture of me, lay my hand on him and tell him I will heal. Then take the message I gave you for your daughter and put it beside it."

You see I did not have a picture of Christopher Reeve, and I said to God, "I have some pictures of Jesus, but no one knows what God looks like. (The Bible says no man can see God's face and live.) He repeated it again, "Take a picture of him and a picture of me, lay my hand on him, and tell him I will heal."

I was getting excited about it, and then in the spirit I saw Christopher Reeve walking. On Monday evening I went back to my doctor's office and asked the receptionist if I could have the article in the magazine. I went home and picked up a picture of Jesus and took the picture of Christopher Reeve. I then went to Kinko's and made a copy of both of them, took the message "I Will Heal" and reduced it down to size of the picture, cut out both of them, moved the dog away from the wheelchair and put Jesus' hand on Mr. Reeve and inserted the message beside them.

At around 6:45 p.m. I left to go to the Von Thomas Women's Ministry meeting, the ministry I was apart of at that time. After the meeting, I asked Von if she would type a letter for me. I had written the foundation, telling them that I was sorry I did not have a donation but this picture had to go to Christopher Reeve. On the following Tuesday I went back to Kinko's and made two copies and had them laminated. I then went to the Post Office with the letter and one of the pictures with the message on it and sent the package to the Christopher Reeve Foundation, certified with a return receipt.

This may sound a little unbelievable to you to do something like this, but I just thank God that chose me when He could have chosen anybody else. You see, I am willing to do whatever He asks me to do. His Word is true, and if He said it, He will do it. You can believe that (As you may say, "You can take it to the bank.") The Bible was actually the first place to come up with the slogan, "Just do it!" In the Bible, which was written more than two thousand years ago, there is a record of Jesus at a wedding. In John 2:5 it says: "His mother said unto the servants, whatsoever he saith unto you, do it."

A MESSAGE FROM THE MASTER

Sometime later I received great encouragement and confirmation from the Lord when a friend told me that she had seen the picture that I had prepared for Christopher Reeve on national television. During a fund-raising program on NBC, Mr. Reeve made reference to the photograph and the poem that had blessed him. My friend reported that he thanked "Deloris Harris from Columbus, Ohio."

Know that God is God, and He can use anybody, if you believe and are willing. God is good all the time. Be encouraged.

www.ingramcontent.com/pod-product-compliance
Lightning Source LLC
Chambersburg PA
CBHW031258290426
44109CB00012B/637